SUPER MARIO ODYSSEY

Kingdom Adventures

Travel Companion Volume 6

Mushroom Kingdom
Dark Side of the Moon
Darker Side of the Moon

Pack Your Bags!

When Mario set out to stop Bowser from forcing Princess Peach to marry him, he had no idea what it would lead to. But his attempt to save a friend quickly proves far more difficult than Mario could have ever anticipated. Much to Peach's dismay, the tuxedo-clad Bowser manages to knock Mario from his ship, sending him tumbling through the night sky.

But to where?

Thanks to a friendly flying top hat known as Cappy, Mario is roused from his slumber in a tiny area of the Cap Kingdom known as Bonneton. The local population isn't just friendly, but they have a stake in stopping Bowser, too! One of their own, Cappy's sister Tiara, was also kidnapped. And he wants to team up with Mario to get her back.

With Cappy's help, Mario soon finds himself in command of the Odyssey, an incredible airship capable of traveling to more than a dozen kingdoms scattered around the globe. From the scorching sands of Tostarena to the bustling streets of New Donk City, there's no place the Odyssey can't go. Don your favorite hat and put your seatback in its full, upright position. The Odyssey is taking flight for Mario's biggest, boldest adventure yet!

Mario's desire to stop Bowser may be his ultimate goal, but the best part of any adventure is the journey, not the destination. And oh, the places you'll go, Mario!

This companion book aims to help you uncover the secrets of three more kingdoms that Mario will visit in his quest. The following pages contain insights into the most popular tourist attractions, regional events and activities, local culture, and souvenirs. Consider this book your ultimate travel buddy, a tour guide designed to not only help you get the most out of your travels, but to also record the memorable times you and Mario share.

This volume provides insights into Mushroom Kingdom, Dark Side of the Moon, and Darker Side of the Moon. For gameplay assistance, maps of Regional Coins and Power Moons, and general strategy, check out the *Official Super Mario Odyssey Strategy Guide*, sold separately.

Mushroom Kingdom

Most Famous of All Kingdoms

They say absence makes the heart grow fonder and that was certainly true for Mario throughout his globetrotting. There was so much to see and do and Mario's horizons were forever broadened, but there's no place like home. While wrapped up in his grand trip, Mario would sometimes feel a little wistful thinking of his faraway homeland. Other visitors who've spent decades adventuring in Mushroom Kingdom will surely feel similar.

The kingdom overseen by Princess Peach is verdant, welcoming, and packed with the useful labor and fun diversions with barely a trace of danger or worry. Toads go about their vocations and avocations with the same sunny disposition and even Uncle amiibo seems more at ease. Take a dip in the pond, explore the vaguely scary woods to the north, mingle at the fountain, and take in the castle grounds.

Apart from famous Mushroom Kingdom folks like Princess Peach, her friend Mario, and his brother Luigi, most people that visitors can expect to encounter are Toads scurrying this way and that, going about their business. Whether in need of help or directions, never hesitate to ask a Toad for assistance.

Aside from the pond, woods, and castle already mentioned (and a sculpted garden, too), the most prominent features are the locked towers standing here and there. Some say these towers staying locked is one reason Mushroom Kingdom is so calm. Entry is generally discouraged except with the permission of the Princess.

Peach's Castle
The elegant heart of the kingdom.

GET TO KNOW PEACH'S CASTLE	
Population	Middling
Size	Wide-ish
Locals	Toads
Currency	64-esque
Industry	Pipes, Tourism
Temperature	Average 81°F

TOADS OF A FEATHER

Few places will you find citizens as warm, friendly, helpful, and industrious as the Toads of Mushroom Kingdom. They are located all over the region, tending to gardens, maintaining tower and castle grounds,  herding sheep, and relaxing around the fountain. Toads make fast friends, happy to loan out motor scooters, let people play with their dogs, and direct visitors toward local points of interest.

THREE KEYS TO THE KINGDOM

 Visit Peach's Castle, the face and heart of the kingdom.

 Relax in the various soothing spots scattered about.

 Stroll through the rolling hills and dales of the castle grounds.

Top Sights

A Lovely Portrait in Glass

Because Princess Peach is so often absent from her kingdom, her citizens took it upon themselves to create a stained-glass portrait of her on the castle balcony. While a pale reflection of the genuine article, the portrait brings comfort to the citizenry when their princess can't be with them.

Mario and his muse. #PrincessPeach #StainedGlass #MushroomKingdom

SCARECROW'S STAIR SHOW

Inspecting the beautiful stained glass up close requires access to the roof, which can be puzzling to figure out. It's a tall castle, after all, and not just anyone should be able to gain entry. After looking around, Mario was able to summit the roof without difficulty, thanks to Cappy. A timer scarecrow west of the castle revealed a magic stairway leading up onto the roof, as long as the Bonneter kept spinning on the scarecrow's head. Cappy was happy to oblige.

Towering Mysteries

In older times, the towers dotting the landscape served as watchtowers. Now they hold and preserve a series of mysterious paintings. These incredibly detailed works are so real that admirers speak of being pulled into another world by the paintings. However, it's extremely rare for tourists to see them due to some undescribed danger and casual visits are discouraged.

PAINTED INTO A CORNER

After Bowser's plot was thwarted and things returned to normal, Mario and Cappy were as antsy to see the world at their leisure as Princess Peach and Tiara. This is why they ended up exploring the magical paintings inside the forbidden old watchtowers of the Mushroom Kingdom. There's a standing soft-ban on locals wandering inside, but Mario is no ordinary son of the Mushroom Kingdom and Cappy is no everyday visitor. Much to their surprise, inside each tower's painting they survived an extra-gnarly encounter with most of the odyssey's biggest, baddest bosses!

It's unclear whether these painting bosses are the real thing, now imprisoned in the paintings after Mario subdued them along his quest or whether they're magical copies. However, the versions of these beasts found here fought much harder than they did before. Only Bowser and the Broodals were excluded from the rematches. (Although that doesn't mean Mario and Cappy never wandered into the Broodal's orbits again. They'd find each other on the dark side of the moon....)

The first selfies were paintings, too. #Painterly #BossTowers #MushroomKingdom

13

Places to Relax

The Toads of the Mushroom Kingdom value their relaxation, having created several lovely spots on the castle grounds for just that purpose. Neither too small nor too large and with just the right amount of ornamentation, these plazas and courtyards exemplify the best traits of this kingdom.

After going all the way there and back again in a global chase with Bowser, Mario and Cappy have earned the right to doze a little.
#ZZZ #FountainRelaxation #MushroomKingdom

DJ MARIO

After a long slog worldwide against Bowser and his forces, Mario had earned plenty of rest and relaxation back home. Among other surprise presents Mario received upon arriving back in Mushroom Kingdom was a music player so he could play whatever background music he liked at anytime.

Music helped propel Mario's entire journey, as his travels exposed him to tunes from all over the globe and several eras, too. Music even took on a physical form, as many timer challenges were initiated by magical music notes.

Mingling with old Toad friends around the fountain and enjoying the calm was a perfect time to try out the new music player. The funky, headphone-wearing Toad is sure to appreciate Mario's catalog, built from the music he's encountered. The music-loving Toad can be found vacationing in other kingdoms too, ready to trade beats with Mario.

Slightly Scary Woods

Even the serene Mushroom Kingdom has its more dangerous locales. This forest was originally planted for mushroom cultivation, but while the mushrooms have flourished, a large number of wild Goombas have taken up residence. While it's come to be known as Goomba Woods, it's still a pleasant place for a stroll. So if you're not afraid of these fearsome beasts, why not treat yourself to a walk?

Leaving Goombas in the dust on a forest joyride!
#ScenicRoute #FuelEfficient #GoombaWoods

GLOB OF GOOMBAS

Goombas are dangerous (kind of) to anyone paying attention. They can also be useful when stacked atop one another and paraded around Mushroom Kingdom. Toad guards scared away (in good fun!) from their posts may reveal hidden secrets. And you'd be surprised at the opportunities to play matchmaker between lonely Goombettes and Goombas. Corralling Goombas is not something just anyone can pull off, though, so bring a friend from Bonneton to help convince the Goombas to stack up.

A Castle's Water Feature

The only lake on the castle grounds features a small but lovely waterfall, making it a popular spot to visit. The lake formed naturally, but some claim that its shape is familiar. Hmm...

MARINE WORLD MUSHROOM KINGDOM

Like any self-respecting watering hole, the lake is surrounded by little diversions. A cross-training Koopa Troopa competitors for Freerunning races, Regional Coins are tucked away in a few waterside nooks and crannies, and a giant, gentle Dorrie drifts on the water's surface. There's even a mysterious Pipe to who-knows-where on the pond's floor and a sealed, off-limits tower to the east in the Odyssey's direction.

Dorrie's got a big head, but always stays humble. #RidingDorrie #TophatTravel #MushroomPond

It's-a-You, Here!

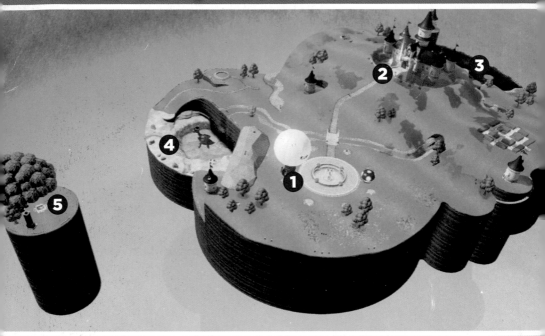

The Odyssey: The crew of the Odyssey sets down not far from a festive fountain located centrally in the kingdom. Mushroom Kingdom unfolds gently to the north of the fountain to the east and west flanks.

Peach's Castle Main Entrance: The bright and welcoming moat of Princess Peach's Castle is a sharp contrast with Bowser's forbidding battlements. Instead of having to infiltrate hostile territory and scale giant walls, anyone is welcome to saunter right up to greet the regal Toad attendants and seek audience with the princess—if she's in! The castle grounds, moat, and rooftop are ripe with apples, coins, and some big surprises.

Goomba Woods: The spooky woods just behind Peach's Castle are home to tons of clumsily aggressive Goombas, who will scamper eagerly after tourists and Toads passing through. Rustic-minded Toads camp on the edges of the forest, enjoying the outdoor spirit without getting overwhelmed by Goomba stacks.

Mushroom Pond: The southwest quad of Mushroom Kingdom dips into a waterlogged quarry. This provides a crystal-clear dipping spot for swimming enthusiasts. A gentle Dorrie floats in the lake, offering a comfortable ride for anyone looking to drift above the tranquil water.

Yoshi's House: Mario and Luigi's dinosaur friend lives a short distance from the Mushroom Kingdom in a cozy hiding spot. The area is usually only accessible through either the magical painting frame located far to the northeast of Mount Volbono, or a checkpoint flag instant warp within Mushroom Kingdom.

Getting Around

The Mushroom Kingdom's landscape is much less disjointed than the fractured paths of many other places. Here, it's mostly grassy hills punctuated in spots by small streams. Getting from place to place never involves more than a decent stroll (and a climb for the castle rooftop or the raised tower in the northwest).

The region's curving hills allow for agile visitors (like Mario, or Shiverians) to roll rapidly across most of the kingdom. There are also Rocket Flowers sprouting in places, allowing temporary rocket-boosted sprints. Use the friendly Toad near the fountain to lend a zippy Motor Scooter to anyone who wants to get around the castle's grounds with maximum ease.

Souvenir Hunting

The Toads of Mushroom Kingdom offer up local trinkets for purple coins only found here, just like in all other populated kingdoms. The exclusive shopkeeper sells more souvenir decals for airships than other kingdoms, rounding out decorations for craft that have been around the world. Even more exciting, though, is the unique blast from the past outfit exclusively sold here. Want to look like you've stepped straight out of 1996's *Super Mario 64*? The Toad outfitter can make it happen!

CRAZY CAP: PEACH'S CASTLE EXCLUSIVES	
ITEM	**REGIONAL COINS**
Pipe Sticker	5
Coin Sticker	5
Block Sticker	5
? Block Sticker	5
Mario 64 Cap	15
Mario 64 Suit	20
Mushroom Kingdom Sticker	10
Mushroom Cushion Set	10
Peach's Castle Model	25

HAZARDS & HOSTILES

Don't expect danger in the orderly and cheerful confines of Mushroom Kingdom unless you seek it out explicitly inside a pipe or tower. Most of the region is so peaceful that a nap in the grass is safe. Sure, divers at the pond must remember to surface for breath and anyone rolling around the edges of the landmass must avoid tumbling off the edges.

Goomba: There's an exception to the peacefulness in the darkened forest in the north behind the castle. These woods are brimming with Goombas, so many that they're making stacks on their own without any Bonneter forcing them to do it first! Thankfully, these little guys don't have the legpower to make it up the hill to the castle moat, nor do they go the long way out of the forest on the sides. They must like the shade of the forest canopy.

Mini Goomba: The yellow immature cousins to full-grown Goombas turn up like motes of dust, knocked out from unswept cubbies in little piles. These aggressive creatures don't stack up and can't be captured.

CAPTIVE FRIENDSHIPS

After so much time spent capturing creatures of the world and putting their abilities to good use, there aren't many creatures to capture around the castle. Most creatures that tourists run into will be friendly and immune to capture: Toads, other tourists, a stray sheep, Koopa Troopas having a friendly race, and so on. There is a memorable, capturable friendly creature here and he's a real doozy for fans new and old!

Yoshi: *The friendly dino is found resting inside an egg on the castle rooftop. Crack the egg open to say hello—it won't hurt him! Toss a willing Bonneter onto Yoshi's head to gain control of him, taking advantage of his flutter jumping and ability to cling to walls and floors with his frog-like tongue. After a nap, Yoshi's always happy to munch on some apples, so take him on a walk and get him fed.*

The Boss Gauntlet, Pt.1

Most citizens stay away from the towers spread throughout the kingdom. No one needs to go anywhere near the eerie paintings locked within, which almost seem to be pulling in anyone who inspects them. But Mario isn't like most citizens. Bolstered by his experience against these creatures, boss fights sprinkled as punctuation on the road to Bowser, he confidently burst into each tower (including the one hidden through a pipe at the bottom of the castle moat) to challenge the foe in each painting.

Another encounter with Bowser was excluded (for that, Mario returned to the Wedding Hall on the moon to enter the fresh painting frames there...) and the Broodals weren't here either (although Mario would see them again soon...). But jazzed-up showdowns with other bosses took place throughout the different paintings in this area.

Torkdrift

The flower-crazed UFO originally seen attempting to suck up all the petals in Wooded Kingdom returned, launching much more dangerous patterns of pulse beams around the room in an effort to uproot Mario.

Knucklotec

Mario had another encounter with the stone slapper from inside the Tostarenan ruins. This time, Knucklotec's attempt to squash Mario with his big fists were augmented

by undead mummies rising from the ground, which forced Mario to step nimbly around a mess of stone and ribbon.

Mechawiggler

For the reprisal of the urban tank battle between Mario driving a Sherm and a Mechawiggler driving, uh, itself, the mysterious painting arranged something twice as fearsome: a tank battle between Mario and *two* Mechawigglers at once!

27

Cookatiel

Inside the painting's replica of the huge Luncheon Kingdom stewpot, Mario had a rematch against the big bird that sent Mount Volbono into critical temperatures stuffing

one in one piece of food too many (an admittedly perfect-looking, jumbo-sized piece of salted meat). The bird seemed to take things much more seriously this time, regurgitating spiked fruit into the soup much faster, while Moonsnakes spun like bladed whisks on the surface, impeding Lava Bubble Mario's movement.

Ancient Dragon

Crumbleden's lord of lightning took another crack at Mario inside the painting hidden in a moat pipe, the only boss rematch here not found in an actual tower. The dragon secured its protective crown with extra stakes and lashed out with more intricate electrical patterns, but Mario and Cappy still prevailed in the end.

Events and Attractions

Archivist Toadette

Archivist Toadette is one of Princess Peach's most reliable assistants. She is always ready at her post right by the Princess's throne, prepared with any facts and figures one might imagine pertaining to Mushroom Kingdom affairs and those of the greater world, too.

With Peach on an extended vacation thanks to Bowser's kidnapping, Archivist Toadette's civic plate for Mushroom Kingdom duties is relatively empty. In the meantime, she kept tabs on all of Mario's accomplishments since Bowser first swept into each kingdom to steal something dear! Anytime Mario and Cappy had a chance to stop by the castle and say hello to the archivist, she'd update them on any new milestones they'd crossed in their questing, doling out invaluable Power Moons for each new achievement!

The Power Moons the Archivist can dole out for achievements increase the number of total moons in Mushroom Kingdom by *over 60*!

Art Appreciation

A magical painting frame can be found here like in most kingdoms. This warp frame is on the ground to the south in a small grove of trees. Depending on the path that world travelers took to arrive here in the Mushroom Kingdom, this frame will display a murky image of a hidden ledge in either Snow Kingdom or Seaside Kingdom. Step through the painting and voila: you're actually there, high above the surroundings in another land.

Toad's Best Friend

This playful pooch has jaunted all over the world, almost as much as Captain Toad or Mario and Cappy! The hat-wearing hound's been spotted in Tostarena, Bubblaine, and even the moon

before hitching a ride with Toad travelers to arrive near Peach's Castle. Here, the dog can get plenty of attention from tourists and Toads, all the while enjoying the lush grass and pleasant sunshine around the fountain. Get its attention and it may lead you to buried secrets around the nearby hills, especially if you play a little fetch!

Mushroom Maze Maintenance

The pride of the castle's landscaping staff, the hedge pattern found in the northeast corner is a gorgeous garden project, the most meticulously maintained foliage in the realm. While Toad is tending the hedges quite well on his own, he could use some help foraging some suitable seeds for fresh pots. Little does he know (perhaps because he's so short and can't see over the hedges), there's a fresh seed located just to the west toward the castle in the little valley. Several other viable seeds can surely be found elsewhere in the kingdom, if not so close by.

Koopa Freerunning

Of all the Freerunning courses, Mushroom Kingdom's is probably the most relaxed. Some seasoned world travelers may find this odd, having arrived in Mushroom Kingdom accomplished runners in other regions, but it's totally in character with the laid-back vibe in Mario's home. From its starting point at Mushroom Pond, lazily watched by the local Dorrie, the route leads away from the pond, then curls toward the castle's bridge. That's it! Rocket Flowers along the way promote maximum speed on this Mushroom Kingdom stroll.

Postcards with Peach

When Princess Peach and Tiara returned to Mushroom Kingdom after their misadventures with Bowser, they took the long way home. They stopped by every other kingdom and experienced their own souvenir-and-outfit collecting adventures. With all the kingdoms being small worlds, Mario and Cappy just happened to run into them at each stop, taking the time to catch up and snap a group pic. After a long time jaunting from one locale to another, they all arrived back home, reminiscing about their sprawling odyssey.

I'll See You on the Dark Side of the Moon...

Mario had been to the actual moon and back, as incredible as that sounds, and returned back home to tell everyone all about it. But it turns out that Mushroom Kingdom wasn't the final surprise. Winding down the chase for Bowser and giving the Koopa king a thorough dethroning had unleashed Moon Cube energy throughout the kingdoms, revealing *hundreds* more Power Moon locations. It's a good thing, too, because the Odyssey needed a lot of fuel to reach the real final frontiers, locations Mario couldn't even chart on navigational maps before he'd amassed 250 Power Moons, then finally 500.

Dark Side of the Moon

Remote Region, Even for the Moon

If the moon was only a hop, skip, jump, and airship ride through space away, the Dark Side of the Moon is only a hop, skip, jump, airship ride, then *another* airship ride away. It's location is well outside the beachhead established by the formation of the Wedding Hall. Being equipped for space travel is rare enough, but having sufficient fuel to travel this far through space is even rarer.

The only actual lands here (the floor of the crater below is too far away to see) are three tall mesas rising up like islands. The old white stone is a tougher landscape than the sands found in less remote regions and the stone mesas are topped with stone veggies to match.

The area itself seems like a treacherous place to live, but the rabbit residents don't seem to mind. Dozens of hares can be found moving throughout the piles of veggies on the central island. This is the rabbit hometown, Rabbit Ridge. Towering nearby, the giant stone carrot structure is the home base of the Broodals, hares who harassed Mario throughout his travels.

finding their home presents a chance to finally go on the offensive.

There are a surprising number of things to do in this relatively small area. Most prominently, there's the rabbits' extensive art collection with clues pointing all over the world. Also, this area contains the most grueling challenge rooms found anywhere.

Rabbit Ridge
The last word in dedicated wedding planning.

GET TO KNOW RABBIT RIDGE	
Population	Unknown
Size	Unknown
Locals	Rabbitish?
Currency	Unknown
Industry	Wedding Planning
Temperature	Unknown

A HARE-RAISING SURPRISE

Now this was unexpected. Deep in a vast moon crater, in a previously uncharted location, a thriving moon village of lunar hares. It was revealed only when Peach was safe and 250 Power Moons were poured into the Odyssey.

The rabbits sure seem related to the scrambling hares found in many other kingdoms, scampering off with hoarded Power Moons. These rabbits are nowhere near as skittish and seem to be content to enjoy their curiously diverse art collection and strange stone vegetables.

THREE KEYS TO THE KINGDOM

1 *Watch out for the moon's light gravity; you can still die by falling off a cliff.*

2 *Search behind all those stone-carved vegetables.*

3 *Greet all four of the keys to this kingdom. You know who they are.*

Top Sights

A Tasty-Looking Tower

This ostentatious stone tower was carved at the direction of the vegetable-loving Madame Broode, who lords over Rabbit Ridge. Her underlings, the Broodals, live within and always have a warm "welcome" for visitors.

The Broodals' home looms in the distance in a shocking new location. #BroodalTower #PrepareForBattle #DarkSide

A Spark Pylon allows crossing between Rabbit Ridge and the Broodals' tower. On the initial visit, only a pylon heading across to a low level can be accessed, but another pylon that leads much higher up in the carrot climb appears later, but only after getting rudely reacquainted with the Broodals.

Topper, Client Relations

Responsible for client relations on behalf of the Broodals' wedding-planning firm, Topper is usually found on-site troubleshooting.

You can tell how serious he is about a battle by the number of hats he has stacked on his head. He doesn't tap into his full hat reserves except for the most dangerous opponents. So if you square off with him and he has lots of hats, you should feel honored...and afraid.

No one stacks hats better than old Topper. No one spins better, either. Few foes can strike as widely as Topper spinning with a big hat stack. #BroodalTopper #TooManyHats #BossGauntlet

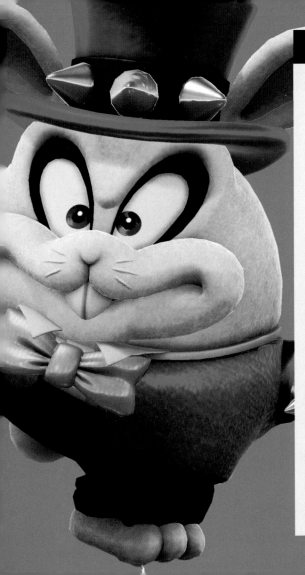

Topper's top hats can be batted aside by thrown objects. When he would flood the arena floor with multiple hats, Mario would throw Cappy with furious speed, over and over, knocking away one Topper hat after another.

Rango, the Bouncer

Although not the most focused, Rango is a valuable player on the Broodals team always coming through in the end. A master of his boomeranging trampoline hat, he can throw it both straight and curved with almost unnatural control. On the other hand, Rango occasionally zones out and looks confused. Take this opportunity to counterattack.

Rango's hats are an extreme cutting hazard along the brim.
#BroodalRango #SawHats #BossGauntlet

HAT TRAMPOLINES

Rango's summer hats may be deadly from the sides or top, but when turned over they reveal a surprisingly plush underside. So plush, in fact, that it replicates the effects of a flower trampoline. Whenever Rango sent his bladed hats spinning after Mario, Mario would flip them with Cappy deflections. Not only did this remove the hat weapons from Rango's clutches temporarily, but it also created platforms for Mario to bounce off.

Hariet, Pyrotechnics

The least predictable of the Broodals, Hariet is most often found throwing bombs with her hair. When her homemade bombs explode, they leave a pool of fire on the ground so try knocking them away before they explode. While it may seem reckless to have filled her hat with bombs, Hariet is devious and keeps a lot of spare explosives with her, so watch out!

Hariet's spiked bombs are extremely hazardous, but they can be deflected back at her before they detonate. #BroodalHariet #BlastHelmet #BossGauntlet

BOMBERWOMAN

Hariet's weapons can be turned against her whether she is spinning morning-star-shaped explosives out on her braids as cudgels, or dropping bombs from inside her flying hat, which is temporarily repurposed as a flying saucer bomber. When she's recoiling from a backfiring explosive, she becomes dazed leaving her noggin exposed for a good stomping. She scrambles around more erratically and quicker than other Broodals when her head is vulnerable, so slow her down by dazing her with another thrown object before moving in for the K.O.

Spewart, the Entertainer

Spinning around while spitting poison in a wide area, Spewart is the least subtle of the Broodals. He also has an unexpectedly artistic side, as his poisonous ground-paintings show.

Spewart must be a really unpleasant vacation partner on airplanes and cruise ships. #BroodalSpewart #PurpleBarf #BossGauntlet

CLEANUP ON THE MOON AISLE

Spewart's main threat is his tendency to restrict an area if he's allowed to spew unchecked. Mario deflected Spewart with hat tosses as the Broodal spun around in a poison-dumping hat and used hat tosses to clean up pools of poison barf when given the chance.

It's-a-You, Here!

The Odyssey: Visiting craft can safely set down on a tall mesa stretching up like its own tower. Stone veggies block a secret door, which is inaccessible unless visitors can somehow convince the ruling Broodals to let them in.

Getting Around

The three landmasses rising from the seemingly endless crater are too far apart to pass between them without the use of Spark Pylons. Spark Pylons allow travel between the region's main landmasses, the landing mesa, the rabbits' village, and the dark carrot tower. Apart from using the pylons to transition between these areas, hoofing it in the moon's low gravity will be the only mode of transport here.

HAZARDS & HOSTILES

Rabbit Ridge is hidden on a tiny series of thin mesas sticking out of the bottom of a gigantic crater with nothing to prevent visitors from tumbling over the sides. There's also the regional oversight of the vicious and scheming Broodals from their nearby tower home. So apart from those things, there's no reason to worry about safety in Rabbit Ridge—sort of.

Low Gravity: By now, anyone visiting Rabbit Ridge has had a few hours of acclimation time getting accustomed to the moon's gravity. Note that gravity is at full-strength inside pipes and caves on the moon. Delving underground, that much closer to the moon's core, must amplify the perception of gravity.

Broodals Mashup: When Mario returned home to the Mushroom Kingdom after a long time spent traveling the world, he discovered many of the bosses he'd encountered now trapped inside special towers in his home kingdom. Here in Rabbit Ridge, he'd run into a more intense boss gauntlet with more personal stakes. The mercenary wedding-planning Broodals

of Rabbit Ridge keenly remembered Mario and how he trounced them. Like the sealed bosses in Mushroom Kingdom, they take the battle here much more seriously than the first time.

The Boss Gauntlet, Pt.2

When Mario rode the Spark Pylon from Rabbit Ridge to the Broodals' tower, he started an arduous climb that would see him forced to fight five boss battles in a row! Madame Broodal isn't present, but all the other Broodals are lined up.

Mario dispatched each Broodal brawler on the way up the carrot tower, hoping the third time would be the charm for each of them (having encountered them all twice before on his journey). They'd reassemble in the Robobrood and take one final crack at Mario at the top.

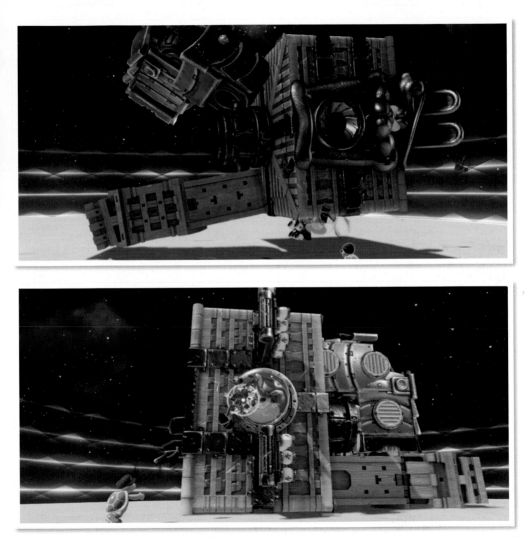

Events and Attractions

Moon Pipe Madness

The Dark Side of the Moon contains Moon Pipes and Scarecrow doors that lead to challenge rooms the likes of which no one has seen back on a full-sized planet. In the lonely isolation of the moon's unexplored corners, the obstacles in these challenge rooms seem to have amplified their difficulty almost out of spite, anticipating the surprise of the rare pathfinders who enter.

These Must Be Very Ripe

One of the most puzzling things about this hidden rabbit village is the generous bounty of stone vegetables. These objects definitely serve at least some capacity as shelter for the rabbits, but it's unknown whether the stone food is also somehow sustenance. Where it came from is also a mystery. It's similar in scale to the oversized produce in Mount Volbono, but whether they're connected is another unanswered question.

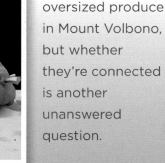

Museum of Modern Moon Art

The unexpected painting collection found here is evidence that the lunar hares are big art fans.

It might also imply another connection between these rabbits and those back home, since the paintings depict specific locations where Power Moons are buried. While some paintings simply depict the location, requiring only that an art student match the background in the territory that inspired the painting, other pieces are actually riddles to solve that point the way to the hidden moon's location.

Ancient Art

Mario found an old glyph on the Dark Side of the Moon that looked a lot like the Cat Peach and Tanooki Mario glyphs he found in each kingdom back home. But this one, which was located near the Spark Pylons leading from Rabbit Ridge to the Broodal tower, depicted Rosalina from *Super Mario Galaxy*!

Darker Side of the Moon

Even More Remote Region

Culmina Crater is twice as difficult to reach as Rabbit Ridge, the hare town located in Dark Side of the Moon. Accessing these landmasses, fingers stretching up from the crater's depths, requires at least 500 Power Moons. Naturally, almost no one has plunged into these depths.

The surface looks like much of the moon in other areas without the action of air and water constantly working over the celestial body's surface. There's just not much variety to find in the surroundings. Underneath the surface, though, is a terrifying cavern system unmatched anywhere in the known solar system. Following the path underground is the only way to explore the surface in Culmina Crater, including the mysterious copy of Metro Kingdom's biggest skyscraper.

Aside from plowing through the fiery underground to arrive at the new New Donk City Hall Tower, there's little to do here. But that stretch in the caverns proves more than enough.

Culmina Crater
Every traveler's final stop.

GET TO KNOW CULMINA CRATER	
Population	Unknown
Size	Unknown
Locals	Unknown
Currency	Unknown
Industry	Unknown
Temperature	Average 73°F

BRING YOUR OWN CITIZENS

Culmina Crater has no natural residents, although whether it ever did is an open question especially with a modern-looking tower in the area. Still, many people have arrived from all over the world to lend Mario their support, including Mayor Pauline and her band!

THREE KEYS TO THE KINGDOM

 1 *See the mysterious building that so closely resembles New Donk City Hall.*

 2 *Reach the far recesses of the giant cavern where none dare tread.*

3 *Test your skills as a hardened tourist one last time.*

Top Sights

One Serious Crater

This giant crater was formed by a huge meteor collision long ago. The impact destroyed the civilization that flourished on the moon, which is how Culmina Crater came to be. The crater is so massive that you cannot see the bottom!

The edges are unforgiving and the drop is bottomless, so watch out! #ToplessMarioTho #BundleUp #CulminaCrater

FROGGY MOON

If you squint, it almost looks like the very first place Mario encountered a Bonneter-capturable enemy way back in Bonneton inside the cap tower. There are a series of ledges along a tall climb and Mario needed to briefly borrow a Frog to do it! Just like back in the cap tower, Frogs are readily found here around a little watering pond. There's water on the moon!

Seeing the Bright Side

From here you can observe galaxies shining in ways you never could from home. Culmina Crater features vistas entirely unique from those you can find on the Dark Side of the Moon and Honeylune Ridge. If you're feeling down or disheartened, just take a look up at the Milky Way from here. You can see each star twinkle as they nestle close to one another.

Compared to all the world's kingdoms (except maybe Crumbleden), the emptiness out here is so stark. Thinking about the scope can be overwhelming. #MarioDeepField #FullofStars #CulminaCrater

It will all be OK— you are not alone.

WITH A LITTLE HELP FROM A FRIEND

Mario took heart because even against the backdrop of endless stars impossibly far away, there's nothing he couldn't accomplish together with Cappy.

A Bewildering Building

This colossal building stands in Culmina Crater. If you look closely, it seems to resemble the city hall in New Donk City. In fact, some think it's based on New Donk City Hall. According to researchers, it might be one of the last remnants of a civilization that once flourished on the moon. But with little evidence, this theory lacks credibility.

It's a strange sight to be sure, but by now odd sights are par for the course. The solar system has anything you can think of! #LunarHall #BeyondtheCaverns #LongJourneysEnd

Why climb it? Because it's there! (Oh, also because there's a Multi-Moon at the very top of the antenna.) The moon's version of City Hall is just as tall as New Donk City's, so Mario needed the help of a Frog yet again to scale the sheer walls.

A Lone Pipe in a Crater

This is the only pipe that connects to the lunar interior. If you find it, we don't recommend jumping right in. What awaits is a trial so harsh it lives up to the name Culmina Crater.

Of course, if you have the confidence of a traveler who has done everything else the world has to offer, give it a shot! Overcome this and adventurers the world over will sing your praises.

Mario, pictured shortly before undertaking the most brutal physical challenge of his life! #TheLastPipe #LastMoonCaveToo #CulminaCrater

To make it through the cavern found inside the pipe, Mario had to use every trick under his cap. His locomotion had to be crisp and error-free and his command of captured creatures convincing. The sprawling cave ended the way it began— with a single pipe connected to the surface, allowing access to the strange tower across the chasm.

Inside the Moon

A lava zone spreads throughout this giant cavern. What waits ahead? How far does it go? These answers await those brave enough to enter this unexplored world.

The cavern stretched out before Mario is much more vast under the ground than the moon's surface.
#MoonCaverns #ADryHeat #CulminaCrater

LUNAR REVUE

Mario and Cappy stayed ready for anything close to the moon's core—and with good reason. Just about anything was required of them at one point or another, ranging from tricky jumps to P-Switch path following to several platforming challenges that required different capturable creatures. With every curveball underground, the heroes remained troupers seeing it through to the end.

It's-a-You, Here!

The Odyssey: Mario's airship sets down gingerly in the sands of the only available spot on the lowest mesa in the kingdom. The platform steps upward several tiers, ending in a small pond opposite the Odyssey.

Getting Around

Like Rabbit Ridge, this is a relatively small lunar area empty of alternate checkpoint flags or vehicles for speeding up travel around the area. Movement must happen on foot, bounding through the moon's low gravity on the surface if desired. (Under the surface, gravity is stronger.) One cluster of mesas is close enough to simply leap between them, but the most distant landmass cannot be reached without crossing through the caves underneath the surface.

HAZARDS & HOSTILES

Outside, there are no hazards except falling off the edge into the crater. Some of the bravest (and wealthiest, apparently, if they could afford the Power Moons to make it here!) fans of Mario from all over the world have traveled here to cheer him on as he approaches the most daunting challenge room of all.

Through the pipe and into the cavern below is a whiplash-inducing contrast. In the cave, it would be easier to list what *isn't* a threat than what is. Basically, solid stone floors and walls are trustworthy and that's about it.

Lava: This is the backdrop for the entire zone, forming a deadly sea underneath everything. It's possible to recover from a fall into the lava in some places, if there's some low platform to reach.

Goomba: These little guys have been ferried across the gulf of space by Yoo-Foe ships and offloaded by these UFOs as a living payload. Their presence can backfire, since a stack of Goombas provides a means to climb up on top of the Yoo-Foe bomber...

Yoo-Foe: This UFO foe flies out of reach of most jumpers from the ground (although Mario can actually make it with the most elite jumping tricks), dumping Goombas and the occasional spiked ball on perceived threats below. This UFO is actually powered by a Life-Up Heart, which is revealed when the ship is destroyed.

Magmato: *Where there is lava, there are Magmatoes. As thin-skinned bags of magma, like water grenades filled with lava, they're not safe to touch and popping them ruins a section of ground with the resulting lava pool. Or, it transforms a bleak and repulsive stretch of hideous dry ground into a refreshing lava hot tub, if you think of it like a Lava Bubble would.*

Burrbo: *These colorful creatures are harmless in small numbers or on open ground where they can easily be brushed aside or dodged. They have an irritating tendency to show up in hordes in the dodgiest of sections, forcing nimble footwork to step around their prickly exteriors.*

Fuzzy: *There's static electricity for the Fuzzies to cluster together invincibly near the core of the moon, too.*

Urban Stingby: *Clouds of Urban Stingbys buzz about in one section of the underground cave, causing horrible problems for the Glydon looking to glide past.*

Donkey Kong: *Mario's original adversary returns for an out-of-this-world rematch!*

CAPTIVE FRIENDSHIPS

With so many openly hostile foes to battle, it's nice to see some friendlier creatures thriving in this inhospitable biome. Like with a similar stretch of an endurance-testing cavern in Moon Kingdom, turning these creatures' presence into an advantage for Mario was the key to pushing through.

Frog: The original jumpmen, Frogs enjoy the low gravity here even more than Mario.

Volbonan: *Maybe the toughest of all the world's peoples, the Volbonans are accustomed to living under an active volcano. A little moon lava doesn't scare them.*

Lava Bubble: *Like Magmatoes, Lava Bubbles are just a natural consequence of pooling enough hot lava in one place. It's a good thing, since Mario needed to go into Lava Bubble form to pass through lava-covered sections of the cave.*

Uproot: *The best climber this side of Pokio with way more upward torque along the way. The stem-growing stretch of an Uproot can push into the underside of loose platforms to raise them.*

Yoshi: *Surprisingly, Mario found Yoshi here! The trusty dino was key to making it past an upward conveyor infested with Fuzzies.*

Glydon: *Everyone's favorite flying lizard is no stranger to steamy places having shown up in Lost Kingdom and Bubblaine before, but this is another level. Surely the intense updrafts here will help the gliding gecko get aloft.*

Pokio: *This feisty little bird packs a mean punch with its beak, which can thrust firmly enough to plant Pokio into sheer vertical surfaces. From each successful plant, the bird can flick itself to the next desired beak-hold.*

Bowser: *Beyond Glydon's glide path and past flicking Volbonan forkfuls of Mario across a lava sea, further still through a pipe leading to a Burrbo dreamland and out again, Mario found a magical painting frame with a very strange image in it. Unlike the warp paintings in many kingdoms or the boss paintings in Mushroom Kingdom, hopping into this painting worked a little differently...*

Events and Attractions

The Final Riddle

The Sphynx really gets around and shows up deep inside the dangerous dungeon. If the Sphynx is after lots of trivia contestants, then this is a terrible place to set up shop. Sphynx at least got to interview the most fun trivia contestant of all, Mario, and rewarded him with a Life-Up Heart for the correct answer.

Galaxy Glyph

Just like in Rabbit Ridge, an ancient glyph of Rosalina can be found. But if this art is old, perhaps dating to an ancient lunar civilization, then why is it on the New Donk City Hall Tower replica? What is going on here?

Show Me the Money

Is the New Donk City Hall Tower here a replica of the one in Metro Kingdom? An antecedent? Who knows, but it definitely hides the solar system's biggest pile of gold coins behind its bulk. The rabbits must have been tucking these away for quite some time, but who stacked them?

79

Kingdom Adventures

Travel Companion Volume 6

Written by Joe Epstein

© 2018 DK/Prima Games, a division of Penguin Random House LLC. Prima Games® is a registered trademark of Penguin Random House LLC. All rights reserved, including the right of reproduction in whole or in part in any form.

The Prima Games logo and Primagames.com are registered trademarks of Penguin Random House LLC, registered in the United States. Prima Games is an imprint of DK, a division of Penguin Random House LLC, New York.

DK/Prima Games, a division of Penguin Random House LLC
6081 East 82nd Street, Suite #400
Indianapolis, IN 46250

© 2018 Nintendo

ISBN: 9780744019353

Printing Code: The rightmost double-digit number is the year of the book's printing; the rightmost single-digit number is the number of the book's printing. For example, 18-1 shows that the first printing of the book occurred in 2018.

21 20 19 18   4 3 2 1

001-310367-Jun/2018

Printed in the USA.

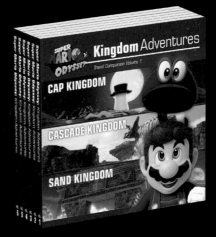